D1539414

Tigers

by Helen Frost

Consulting Editor: Gail Saunders-Smith, Ph.D.

Consultants: Tammy Quist, President,
The Wildcat Society

Pebble Books

an imprint of Capstone Press
Mankato, Minnesota

Pebble Books are published by Capstone Press
151 Good Counsel Drive, P.O. Box 669, Mankato, Minnesota 56002
http://www.capstone-press.com

1 2 3 4 5 6 07 06 05 04 03 02

Library of Congress Cataloging-in-Publication Data
Frost, Helen, 1949–
    Tigers / by Helen Frost.
    p. cm.—(Rain forest animals)
    Summary: Simple text and photographs present the features and behavior
of tigers.
    Includes bibliographical references (p. 23) and index.
    ISBN 0-7368-1458-2 (hardcover)
    1. Tigers—Juvenile literature. [1. Tigers. 2. Rain forest animals.] I. Title.
QL737.C23 F763 2003
599.756—dc21   2002001231

Note to Parents and Teachers

The Rain Forest Animals series supports national science standards
related to life science. This book describes and illustrates tigers that
live in tropical rain forests. The photographs support early readers
in understanding the text. The repetition of words and phrases
helps early readers learn new words. This book also introduces
early readers to subject-specific vocabulary words, which are
defined in the Words to Know section. Early readers may need
assistance to read some words and to use the Table of Contents,
Words to Know, Read More, Internet Sites, and Index/Word List
sections of the book.

Table of Contents

Tigers are big, wild cats.
Cats are mammals.

Most tigers are orange.
They have black stripes.

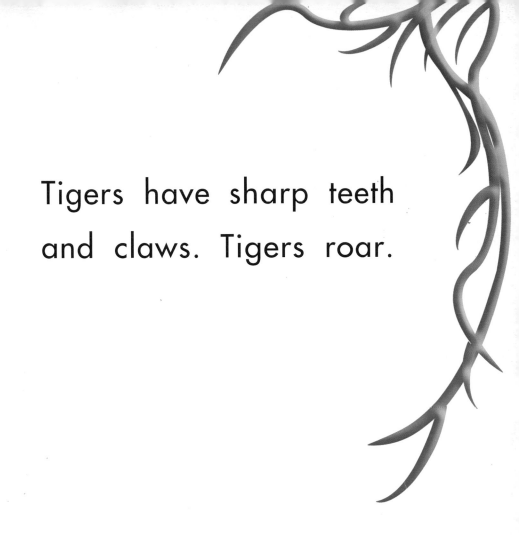

Tigers have sharp teeth and claws. Tigers roar.

places tigers live

Some tigers live
in the rain forests
of southern Asia.

emergent layer

canopy layer

understory layer

forest floor

Tigers prowl along
the forest floor.
Most tigers live alone.

Tigers sometimes swim
in rivers or lakes.

15

Tiger cubs live
with their mother. She
teaches them to hunt.

18

Tigers hunt at night.
They pounce
on their prey.

Tigers sleep in the shade during the day.

Words to Know

Asia—the largest continent on the earth; tigers live in India and several countries in southeast Asia.

cat—an animal with sharp claws and whiskers; tigers are wild cats; lions, jaguars, and cheetahs are also wild cats.

cub—a young tiger; tiger cubs stay with their mother for about two years.

forest floor—the bottom layer of the rain forest; almost no sunlight reaches the forest floor.

mammal—a warm-blooded animal with a backbone; mammals feed milk to their young.

pounce—to jump on something suddenly

prey—an animal that is hunted by another animal for food; a tiger's prey includes deer, antelope, wild pigs, and porcupines.

prowl—to move around quietly and secretly

rain forest—a thick area of trees where rain falls almost every day; some tigers live in rain forests; other tigers live in the mountains.

Read More

Middleton, Don. *Tigers.* Big Cats. New York: PowerKids Press, 1999.

Richardson, Adele. *Tigers: Striped Stalkers.* The Wild World of Animals. Mankato, Minn.: Bridgestone Books, 2002.

Welsbacher, Anne. *Tigers.* Wild Cats. Edina, Minn.: Abdo Publishing Company, 2000.

Internet Sites

Creature Feature: Tigers
http://www.nationalgeographic.com/kids/creature_feature/0012

Tiger (Panthera Tigris)
http://www.panda.org/kids/wildlife/mntiger.htm

Tiger
http://www.wildcatsociety.org/catalog/big%20cats/tiger.html

Index/Word List

alone, 13
Asia, 11
black, 7
cats, 5
claws, 9
cubs, 17
day, 21
forest floor,
  13
hunt, 17, 19

lakes, 15
mammals, 5
mother, 17
night, 19
orange, 7
pounce, 19
prey, 19
prowl, 13
rain forests,
  11

rivers, 15
roar, 9
shade, 21
sharp, 9
sleep, 21
stripes, 7
swim, 15
teaches, 17
teeth, 9
wild, 5

Word Count: 79
Early-Intervention Level: 11

Editorial Credits

Martha E. H. Rustad, editor; Linda Clavel and Heidi Meyer, cover designers; Jennifer Schonborn, interior illustrator; Angi Gahler, book designer; Wanda Winch, photo researcher; Karen Risch, product planning editor

Photo Credits

Bruce Coleman Inc./Erwin and Peggy Bauer, 18; Tom Brakefield, 1, 4
Digital Vision, 10
Photo Network/Mark Newman, 6, 20
Ralf Schmode, 8
Tom and Pat Leeson, cover, 14
Visuals Unlimited/Tom Uhlman, 16

The author thanks the children's section staff at the Allen County Public Library in Fort Wayne, Indiana, for research assistance.